PT Boats

by Michael Green

Consultant:
Alyce Guthrie
Executive Vice President
PT Boats, Inc.

CAPSTONE
HIGH/LOW BOOKS
an imprint of Capstone Press
Mankato, Minnesota

Capstone High/Low Books are published by Capstone Press
818 North Willow Street • Mankato, MN 56001
http://www.capstone-press.com

Library of Congress Cataloging-in-Publication Data
Green, Michael, 1952-
    PT boats/by Michael Green.
        p. cm. — (Land and sea)
    Includes bibliographical references and index.
    Summary: Describes the history, design, weapons, and tactics of the
torpedo-carrying PT boats, used chiefly during World War II.
    ISBN 0-7368-0042-5
    1. Torpedo-boats—United States—Juvenile literature.
[1. Torpedo boats.] I. Title. II. Series: Land and sea (Mankato, Minn.)
V833.G74 1999
359.8'358'0973—dc21

                                                        98-15239
                                                           CIP
                                                            AC

Editorial credits
Matt Doeden, editor; James Franklin, cover designer and illustrator;
    Sheri Gosewisch, photo researcher
Photo credits
Department of Defense, 13
The John F. Kennedy Library, 35
PT Boats, Inc., cover, 4, 40
U.S. Navy, 7, 8, 11, 14, 16, 18, 21, 22, 24, 26, 28, 30, 36, 38, 47

Table of Contents

Chapter 1

PT Boats

Patrol torpedo boats (PT boats) were small fighting boats. The U.S. Navy used them during World War II (1939–1945). PT boats carried explosives called torpedoes. Torpedoes travel underwater to destroy enemy warships. PT boats were fast. Their speed and torpedoes made them a danger to enemy warships.

Some people called PT boats mosquito boats. PT boats reminded people of mosquitoes because the boats were so small. PT boats could sneak up on enemies and attack them quickly.

PT boats were small fighting boats.

Size and Speed

The first torpedo boat was only 15 feet (4.6 meters) long. It was faster than large warships. People measure the speed of ships and boats in knots. One knot equals 1.15 miles (1.85 kilometers) per hour. Early torpedo boats traveled at about 25 knots. They had steam-powered engines. But these torpedo boats were not PT boats yet.

The U.S. Navy used true PT boats during World War II. These boats were between 70 and 80 feet (21 and 24 meters) long. They weighed from 40 to 51 tons (36 to 46 metric tons). They could travel at speeds of up to 45 knots.

Safety

The U.S. Navy did not build PT boats for safety. It built the boats for speed. PT boats had light, wooden hulls. A hull is the main body of a ship or boat. PT boats also had engines that ran on gasoline. The gasoline

PT boats had wooden hulls.

often caught fire during battles. Fires could spread to the wooden hulls. This put PT boat crews in danger.

PT boats had some safety features. They carried fire extinguishers to help crew members put out fires. Some PT boats carried rubber life rafts. The rafts allowed crew

PT boats had no armor.

members to escape from boats that caught fire.
They also allowed crew members to escape
from sinking boats.

PT boats had no armor. This protective
metal covering would have slowed down PT

boats. PT boats sank easily if enemies shot them. Crew members on PT boats watched for enemies carefully. PT boats usually could speed away from enemy warships. Few PT boats sank because of enemy fire.

Crews

A PT boat crew ranged in size from 10 to 16 people. The commander of the boat was the skipper. The second in charge was the executive officer (XO). The XO took over the boat if the skipper could not command any more.

A crew also included a quartermaster, one or two torpedomen, and two or three motor machinist mates. The quartermaster steered the boat. The torpedomen handled and launched the torpedoes. The motor machinist mates kept the boat's engines and equipment working.

Most PT boats also had crew members to operate devices such as guns, radio, and radar. Radar uses radio waves to locate and guide objects. Each crew member had to be able to do every job. They had to be ready to take over other jobs if another crew member became wounded.

Most PT boats had crew members to operate the guns.

Tactics

PT boat crews used surprise tactics to attack enemy ships. Crews attacked mainly at night. They often moved close to large warships without being spotted. But night attacks were not always safe. Many enemy ships had spotlights. Enemy crews sometimes could see a PT boat's wake. A wake is the water turned up by a moving boat.

Early torpedoes were slow. PT boat crews had to move their boats near enemy ships before they launched their torpedoes. Sometimes PT boat crews waited for enemy ships to pass nearby. Then they launched torpedoes and sped away before the enemy could fight back. Sometimes crew members used smoke to hide their boats from enemies. They also used smoke to cover their attacks on enemies.

Destroyers

Destroyers were the biggest danger to the first PT boats. Destroyers are long, slender

Destroyers are long, slender warships.

warships. Navies built the first destroyers to battle early torpedo boats. The navies called them torpedo boat destroyers. Navies later shortened this name to destroyers.

By World War II, navies used destroyers mainly to fight large warships. Destroyers were not as big a danger to PT boats.

Chapter 2

Weapons

Crews on PT boats had many weapons. They used guns, cannons, and missiles. Early crews depended most heavily on torpedoes. Weapons such as missiles became more important by the end of World War II.

Torpedoes

A torpedo has two main parts. The warhead is the part of a missile or torpedo that carries explosives. The other part contains the propeller and the motor. A propeller is a set of rotating blades that pushes an object through the water.

Early PT boat crews depended heavily on torpedoes.

Early PT boats had Mark 8 torpedoes. Mark 8 torpedoes were about 20 feet (6 meters) long. They weighed 2,600 pounds (1,179 kilograms). Mark 8 torpedoes were slow. They traveled at about 27 knots.

PT boats carried large torpedo tubes. Crews needed the tubes to launch Mark 8 torpedoes. The tubes were heavy. They slowed down PT boats.

In 1943, the U.S. Navy began arming PT boats with a new kind of torpedo. It was the Mark 13 torpedo. These torpedoes were lighter than Mark 8 torpedoes. They hit enemy ships more often than Mark 8 torpedoes did. They did not require large torpedo tubes. This made PT boats lighter and faster.

Depth Charges

Most PT boats carried between two and four depth charges. A depth charge is a large

Early PT boats carried large torpedo tubes.

metal can filled with explosives. Crews dropped depth charges into the water to attack enemy submarines that traveled below the ocean's surface.

PT boat crew members dropped depth charges over the edges of their boats. Depth charges weighed more than 400 pounds (181 kilograms). They sank to a set depth. Then they would explode. Each depth charge had a device that made it explode at a different depth.

Machine Guns

Most PT boats carried four machine guns. The guns were in turrets. A turret is a mount for a gun. Each PT boat had two turrets. Each turret held two guns. There was one turret on each side of the boat. Some PT boat crews

Machine guns on PT boats were in turrets.

carried extra machine guns. But the weight of the guns slowed down the boats.

The machine guns on PT boats could fire 600 bullets per minute. The guns could swing all the way around. They could point nearly straight up. But machine guns had short ranges. They were not powerful enough to destroy armored objects.

Crew members used machine guns mainly against other small boats and barges. The Japanese military used barges to carry supplies from island to island in the Pacific Ocean.

Cannons and Rockets

Some PT boats had cannons. The cannons shot shells. The shells were larger than bullets. PT boats usually had cannons on their front ends. Crew members used cannons to destroy armored targets.

Each machine gun turret held two guns.

PT boats usually had cannons on their front ends.

Some PT boats carried 37-millimeter cannons. These cannons shot 120 shells per minute. But 37-millimeter cannons did not work well against aircraft. They did not have a long enough range.

PT boats rarely fought aircraft. But the navy still armed some PT boats with 40-millimeter cannons. These cannons shot 160 shells per minute. They were more effective against enemy aircraft than 37-millimeter cannons were. They had a greater range.

Sometimes even 40-millimeter cannons were not powerful enough to destroy enemy aircraft and warships. The navy armed some of its PT boats with explosive rockets. Rockets had longer ranges than any other PT boat weapon. Rockets also caused large amounts of damage when they hit enemy aircraft and ships.

Radio Antenna

Machine Gun Turret

Radar

Torpedo Tubes

Cockpit

PT Boat

Machine Gun

Hull

Chapter 3

Torpedo Boat History

The British Navy built the first steam-powered torpedo boat in 1877. The British Navy called it the *HMS Lightning*. Later, other navies built steam-powered torpedo boats. But these boats broke down easily.

Torpedo boats powered by gasoline engines replaced steam-powered boats during the early 1900s. Navies called these boats motor torpedo boats (MTBs). The U.S. Navy renamed these boats PT boats.

The U.S. Navy gave motor torpedo boats the name PT boats.

U.S. Navy PT Boats

During the mid-1930s, the U.S. Navy had no PT boats. But navy leaders knew there might be war against the Japanese military. The Japanese military was building a fleet of new warships. The U.S. Navy ordered more than 500 PT boats for itself. It ordered more PT boats for its allies. Allies are countries that work together.

A company called the Electric Boat Company (Elco) built the first PT boats for the U.S. Navy. The company built 77-foot (23-meter) PT boats. They weighed 46 tons (42 metric tons). Their top speed was 42 knots. The boats carried crews of 10 people.

Elco also built 80-foot (24-meter) PT boats. These boats weighed from 51 to 61 tons (46 to 55 metric tons). They carried crews of 11 to 17 people. They were faster than earlier PT boats. Their top speed was 43 knots.

The U.S. Navy ordered more than 500 PT boats during World War II.

Elco built many PT boats for the U.S. Navy.

Higgins Industries and Huckins Yacht
Company built 78-foot (23.5-meter) PT boats.
Higgins PT boats weighed from 43 to 48 tons
(39 to 44 metric tons). They carried crews of
11 to 17 people. Their top speed was 40 knots.
Huckins PT boats weighed 42 tons (38 metric

tons). They carried crews of 10 people. Their top speed was 40 knots.

Missions

The U.S. Navy used PT boats for several kinds of missions. PT boat crews fought in battles. They also went on scouting missions. They searched island coastlines for enemy ships. PT boats carried important military officials. Crews rescued pilots whose planes had been shot down. They even picked up and dropped off military spies.

Many PT boat missions were dangerous. Enemy aircraft could drop bombs on PT boats. Enemy destroyers sometimes hunted PT boats. One of the biggest dangers to PT boats was shallow water. The boats could sink if they hit objects that were close to the ocean's surface. Strips of rock or coral called reefs were one danger to PT boats. Almost

World War II Naval Battles of the Pacific Ocean

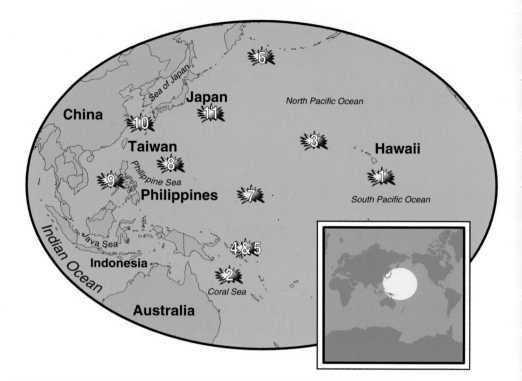

1. Pearl Harbor,
   Dec. 7, 1941
2. Battle of the Coral Sea,
   May 4-8, 1942
3. Battle of Midway,
   June 3-6, 1942
4. Guadalcanal Campaign,
   Aug. 1942 to Feb. 1943
5. Northern Solomons Campaign,
   Feb. 22, 1943 to Nov. 21, 1944
6. Battle of the Komandorski Islands,
   Mar. 26, 1943

7. Truk Attack,
   Feb. 17-18, 1944
8. Battle of the Philippine Sea,
   June 19-20, 1944
9. Leyte Campaign,
   Oct. 17, 1944 to July 1, 1945
10. Sinking of the *Yamato,*
    Apr. 7, 1945
11. Destruction of the Japanese Navy,
    July 10 to Aug. 15, 1945

70 PT boats sank during World War II. A total of 331 crew members died.

John F. Kennedy

The most famous PT boat crew member was John F. Kennedy. Kennedy was president of the United States between 1961 and 1963. Kennedy commanded a PT boat during World War II. He took command of the boat PT-109 in April 1943.

In August 1943, a Japanese destroyer rammed PT-109. Two of the 13 crew members died. Kennedy and the others were wounded. They were in the water for many hours. But they swam to the closest island. Kennedy helped a wounded crew member reach the shore.

The crew members waited to be rescued. They ate coconuts to stay alive. But rescue boats did not come. Kennedy swam to another island to find help. He found someone who could contact the U.S. Navy. The navy rescued the crew members several days later.

Many people thought Kennedy was a hero for saving his crew. The U.S. Navy gave him two medals. One was the Navy and Marine Corps Medal. The other was the Purple Heart. People admired Kennedy's actions in the war. In 1960, voters elected him president of the United States.

The U.S. Navy gave John F. Kennedy two medals for his actions in World War II.

Chapter 4

PT Boats after World War II

The U.S. Navy had hundreds of PT boats after Japan surrendered in 1945. The navy had no use for the boats once the war was finished. Most of the boats were old and worn out.

The navy scrapped many of its PT boats after World War II. It took useful parts such as guns off the boats. Then it burned the boats.

The navy sent some PT boats to its allies. It sold other boats to civilians. A civilian is a person who is not in the military.

The U.S. Navy sent some PT boats to its allies.

Aluminum PT Boats

The U.S. Navy was building aluminum PT boats when World War II ended in 1945. Aluminum is a light, silver-colored metal. But manufacturers did not finish these boats before the war ended.

The navy kept the aluminum PT boats until 1959. They were larger and faster than wooden PT boats. But in 1959, navy leaders decided there was no longer a need for PT boats. The navy scrapped the aluminum boats.

PT Boats Today

Civilians bought used PT boats for different reasons. Some people used them as fishing boats. Others used them as ferry boats to carry people from place to place.

Today, most PT boats are too old to be useful. Some groups restore PT boats to their original condition. These groups find PT boats

The navy was building aluminum PT boats when World War II ended in 1945.

Some naval museums display restored PT boats.

the navy sold. Group members try to make
the boats look just as they did during World
War II.

Some naval museums display restored
PT boats. Two PT boats are at Battleship Cove
in Fall River, Massachusetts. Visitors to this
museum can learn about PT boat history.

Words to Know

allies (AL-eyes)—countries that work together

aluminum (uh-LOO-mi-nuhm)—a light, silver-colored metal

armor (AR-mur)—a protective metal covering

civilian (si-VIL-yuhn)—a person who is not in the military

depth charge (DEPTH CHARJ)—a metal can filled with explosives

fleet (FLEET)—a group of warships under one command

knot (NOT)—a measurement of speed for ships; one knot equals 1.15 miles (1.85 kilometers) per hour.

launch (LAWNCH)—to send into action

missile (MISS-uhl)—an explosive that travels long distances through the air

mission (MISH-uhn)—a military task
propeller (pruh-PEL-ur)—a set of rotating blades that pushes an object through the water
radar (RAY-dar)—machinery that uses radio waves to locate and help guide objects
restore (ri-STOR)—to bring back to an original condition
submarine (SUHB-muh-reen)—a warship that can run on the surface of the water or underwater
tactic (TAK-tik)—a plan for fighting a battle
torpedo (tor-PEE-doh)—an explosive that travels underwater
turret (TUR-it)—a mount for a gun
wake (WAYK)—the water turned up by a moving boat
warhead (WOR-hed)—the part of a missile or torpedo that carries explosives

To Learn More

Asimov, Isaac and Elizabeth Kaplan. *How Do Big Ships Float?* Ask Isaac Asimov. Milwaukee: Gareth Stevens, 1993.

Green, Michael. *Destroyers.* Land and Sea. Mankato, Minn.: Capstone High/Low Books, 1999.

Green, Michael. *The United States Navy.* Serving Your Country. Mankato, Minn.: Capstone High/Low Books, 1998.

Useful Addresses

Battleship Cove
Fall River, MA 02721

Naval Historical Center
Washington Navy Yard
901 M Street SE
Washington, DC 20374-5060

PT Boats, Inc.
P.O. Box 38070
Memphis, TN 38183-0070

Internet Sites

JFK—The War Hero
http://www.historyplace.com/kennedy/
   warhero.htm

Knights of the Sea
http://www.geocities.com/Pentagon/4017/
   rjwapt01.html

PT Boats, Inc.
http://www.geocities.com/Pentagon/6140

U.S. Navy History
http://www.history.navy.mil

Index